dimensional
MACHINE embroidery

10+ SPECIALTY TECHNIQUES
for AMAZING RESULTS

Deborah Jones

kp

KRAUSE PUBLICATIONS
CINCINNATI, OHIO

DISTRIBUTED IN CANADA BY FRASER DIRECT
100 Armstrong Avenue
Georgetown, ON, Canada L7G 5S4
Tel: (905) 877-4411

DISTRIBUTED IN THE U.K. AND EUROPE BY DAVID & CHARLES
Brunel House, Newton Abbot, Devon, TQ12 4PU, England
Tel: (+44) 1626 323200, Fax: (+44) 1626 323319
Email: postmaster@davidandcharles.co.uk

DISTRIBUTED IN AUSTRALIA BY CAPRICORN LINK
P.O. Box 704, S. Windsor NSW, 2756 Australia
Tel: (02) 4577-3555

Library of Congress Cataloging in Publication Data
Jones, Deborah (Deborah Hurd-Jones)
Dimensional machine embroidery : 10 specialty techniques for amazing results / Deborah Jones. -- 1st ed.
    p. cm.
  Includes index.
  ISBN-13: 978-1-4402-0397-8 (pbk. : alk. paper)
  ISBN-10: 1-4402-0397-0 (pbk. : alk. paper)
  1. Embroidery, Machine. I. Title.
  TT772.J657 2010
  746.44028--dc22
                                2010004752

Editors: Jennifer Claydon and Rachel Scheller
Designer: Julie Barnett
Production Coordinator: Greg Nock
Photographers: Christine Polomsky, Ric Deliantoni
Stylist: Nora Martini

METRIC CONVERSION CHART

to convert	to	multiply by
inches	centimeters	2.54
centimeters	inches	0.4
feet	centimeters	30.5
centimeters	feet	0.03
yards	meters	0.9
meters	yards	1.1

DEDICATION

This book is lovingly dedicated to my late husband,
Bob Hurd, who always supported my embroidery,
and to Dee Hitzfelder, who hung the moon.

ABOUT THE AUTHOR

Deborah Jones has been sharing her embroidery knowledge with her fellow embroiderers for decades. Her family owned a tailoring business that used automated embroidery machines as early as the 1960s. She has traveled internationally teaching embroidery techniques.

Deborah writes the "Ask the Expert" column for *Designs in Machine Embroidery* magazine and the "Technically Speaking" column for *Stitches* magazine. Her expertise ranges from design creation and techniques at the machine to starting an embroidery business. She assists embroiderers through her Web site, www.myembroiderymentor.com.

Deborah lives in her rural home outside Dallas, Texas, where she trains embroiderers and creates video lessons in her embellishment studio.

ACKNOWLEDGMENTS

Thanks to:

Opal McCleary and Dee Hitzfelder, who helped
with sewing aspects of the projects.

My friend Lois Lizza, who always
gives me a different perspective.

Jackie Woods for her support.

Suzanne Hinshaw, for providing
her beautiful shadow work designs.

My editors, Rachel Scheller
and Jennifer Claydon.

Christine Polomsky, whose photography
skills made this book possible.

Christine Doyle for her appreciation
of the concept of this book.

Harry Jay and Mike Woodull for creating
the artwork for the embroidery designs.

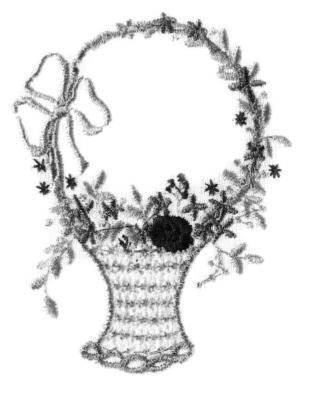

CONTENTS

AN OVERVIEW OF
Dimensional Techniques

By its very nature, embroidery of any kind is dimensional, with thread rising above a base fabric to add character and depth. Indeed, its dimensional aspect is likely the most elemental part of embroidery's appeal. Ordinary fabrics become extraordinary, stories are told and inspiration takes tangible form through needle and thread. For centuries, we have continued to improve the techniques and technology to accomplish embroidery in many forms. In this book, we will explore an approach to embroidery that goes beyond the basics. These techniques can be a springboard for your own approach to taking embroidery to new heights.

DEFINING DIMENSIONAL EMBROIDERY

For the purpose of explaining the criteria for selecting methods to include in this book, I should first give my definition of dimensional machine embroidery. For me, a dimensional embroidery technique is one that has an added element. This could be an added technique or ingredient, such as hand-painted details or quilt batting. It could incorporate the use of a special needle to make small holes or eyelets in the fabric during the course of embroidering. Threads may be clipped to create fringe, or shiny Mylar may be placed under embroidery stitching to give a shimmering metallic glow.

This collection of projects includes some of my favorites. I have used more than one dimensional technique in a few. Combining techniques sometimes leads to the creation of a real showpiece, while other times the result may be a subtle but intriguing effect that draws the eye.

Many of the techniques covered are traditional techniques that can be adapted to machine embroidery, including computerized machine embroidery. For me, dimensional embroidery can be rich

and inviting without being outlandish or over the top. Still, the techniques allow for plenty of artistic license, and realism may go out the window in favor of a fun and fanciful interpretation of a theme.

Some dimensional embroidery techniques can be accomplished by using designs that you already have in your library. Throughout the book, I will point out design editing methods that may be used to adapt your existing designs to specific techniques. Additionally, the included DVD contains all of the designs used in the projects. This makes it possible not only for you to stitch them yourself, but also to examine the designs in embroidery software and see them in the various settings and parameters used to create these special effects.

When creating dimensional embroidery, we are often mixing nonstandard components with our embroidery. It is important to carefully evaluate the characteristics of each component for compatibility with the others. For example, we can't mix recommended fabric care types, such as a wash-only fabric with a dry-clean-only fabric.

I feel adventurous when working on dimensional embroidery projects. I may have a good idea of the anticipated result, yet I sometimes have a happy accident that takes the project in a completely different direction. Keep this in mind when working on your own dimensional embroidery; you may develop new and interesting techniques of your own.

Feeling adventurous? The possibilities for dimensional embroidery are many and limited only by our imaginations. I encourage you to read this book, select your favorite projects to create and then expand on the ones you like best.

Faux Trapunto
Paint sticks and a layer of batting inserted beneath the fabric add dimension to a simple running stitch pattern.

MACHINE AND SUPPLY REQUIREMENTS

The projects in this book have been designed for use with a computerized embroidery machine. With just a couple of exceptions, the projects contained here include versions for use with hoops as small as 4" × 4" (10.2cm × 10.2cm). There are no special equipment requirements except the ability to get the designs from the included DVD to your embroidery machine. This can be accomplished by transferring the designs directly from the DVD to a memory device accepted by your machine, such as a flash drive or memory card. Other machines allow transfer directly from the computer to the machine through a cable.

Recommended colors for the designs are listed with a descriptive name and color number for the Sulky thread brand in the stitching guides accompanying each project. (A PDF file of each stitching guide is also included on the DVD.) Color numbers

can be converted to other thread brands at Web sites listed in the Resources section of this book. Recommended stabilizers are also listed by type in the relevant chapter, with detailed information in the Resources section.

Be sure to watch the instructional video included in the DVD. It's a great resource that provides an indepth look at each of the techniques and includes hints and tips for success. You'll join Nancy and me as we create projects in this book. Watch our techniques and hear our insights about the processes as they happen. The video can be watched in any standard DVD player, or on a computer that has DVD-playing capabilities.

Traditional and Raw-Edge Appliqué
EASY ELEGANCE

Appliqué has been with us for centuries, with hand-embroidery artisans carefully folding back fabric edges and securing them with tiny, carefully placed stitches. This meticulous process can be translated to a computerized embroidery method to create appliqués in a fraction of the time and with similar precision.

TRADITIONAL and RAW-EDGE APPLIQUÉ

materials

Towel

Felted wool (in two colors for raw-edge technique)

Light-tack fusible tear-away stabilizer

Self-adhesive tear-away stabilizer

Rayon, cotton or polyester embroidery thread

Standard embroidery needles

Sharp, short-blade scissors

Iron and ironing board

5" × 7" (12.7cm × 17.8cm) embroidery hoop if using FleurDeLys and Fleur_Raw_Edge designs

4" × 4" (10.2 ×10.2) embroidery hoop if using Fleur_Raw_Small design

Fleur-de-lys embroidery designs (01_FleurDeLys, 01_Fleur_Raw_Edge and 01_Fleur_Raw_Small)

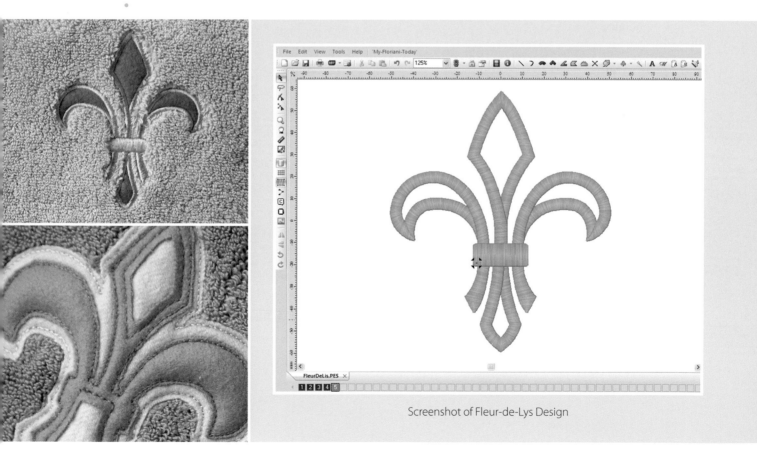

Screenshot of Fleur-de-Lys Design

RECOMMENDATIONS

FABRIC

This project calls for felted wool. This type of wool is washable because it has already been subjected to water and heat. You can purchase felted wool or make your own. There are several Web sites that give instructions on making wool felt. It can be made from wool fibers or old wool blankets and sweaters. You can complete the project with any kind of washable felt, but wool felt is the richest in appearance and will hold up best to washing and regular use.

STABILIZERS

For holding the towel in the hoop, we will use two types of specialty stabilizers. The first is a light-tack fusible, such as Totally Stable from Sulky. This will serve as a buffer between the towel and the aggressive adhesive of the self-adhesive tear-away stabilizer. Its gentle hold will not pull or damage the loops of the towel. The fusible stabilizer covers the embroidery area and contacts the hooped self-adhesive stabilizer.

THREAD

The type of thread that you use depends on the finished look that you want. Cotton thread will give a matte finish, and polyester or rayon will look shiny. Polyester is the best choice if you use detergent that contains bleach.

SCISSORS

The appliqué piece will be trimmed after it has been stitched. This is most easily accomplished with short-blade embroidery scissors with sharp blades and tips. Some embroiderers find it helpful to use scissors with curved blades. I find it easiest to maneuver when the overall scissor length is 5" (12.7cm) or less.

NOTES FROM **NANCY**

When considering stabilizers for embroidery projects, my mantra is "more is better!" Bottom stabilizers give substance to the base fabric, and top stabilizers allow the embroidery to "sit" on top of the fabric. The result—a professional project.

Towels with Washable Wool Felt Fleur-de-Lys

If you have ever had an appliqué project that didn't quite work out because the fabric raveled or wrinkled, you will be happy to know that these possibilities don't exist with this project. Felt doesn't ravel because it isn't a woven fabric, and its firm body will not allow it to wrinkle on the cushioned surface of the towel. For the raw-edge technique, you will need two colors of felted wool.

HOOPING THE FABRIC

Most home embroidery hoops have narrow sides, making it difficult to hold thick towels securely. This holding technique works well for bulky towels with an added bonus: no hoop marks! I recommended it for both the traditional and raw-edge appliqué techniques.

2 Iron a light-tack fusible tear-away stabilizer to the wrong side of the towel.

3 Mark the center of the towel. Secure the towel to the hoop by placing the tear-away stabilizer down on the self-adhesive stabilizer. The design should be positioned approximately 1½ " (3.8cm) above the decorative border on the towel.

1 Hoop a piece of self-adhesive stabilizer. Score the backing paper and remove it from the interior of the hoop.

TIP The fusible tear-away stabilizer protects the towel from the aggressive adhesive on the self-adhesive stabilizer.

TRADITIONAL APPLIQUÉ

Although you can hoop your towel in the conventional manner in a two-ring hoop for this project, I recommend using the self-adhesive method described on page 15. Two-ring hoops for home machines have narrow sides—a thick towel can easily pop out. The hoop must be removed from the machine for trimming and then reinserted without disturbing the position of the towel. You certainly don't want the towel to pop out of the hoop during this step.

1 Stitch the running-stitch target for the appliqué directly on the towel. Cover the target stitch with the appliqué fabric, making sure that the fabric extends beyond the stitching.

2 Stitch the first design stitch, a running stitch. After stitching, remove the hoop very carefully from the machine. Take care that you don't disturb the position of the towel.

Trim the felt close to the cutting line. Your cutting technique is the key to success here. You must cut closely so you don't have felt extending beyond the satin stitch. Practice using a gliding motion rather than opening and closing the blades. A gliding motion gives a smoother cut than a cutting motion, but it requires very sharp blades. No matter how you do it, get as close to the cutting line as possible without disturbing the position of the towel.

3 Finish embroidering the design. Each section will start with tackdown stitches, followed by the final satin stitch.

RAW-EDGE APPLIQUÉ

This is the easiest appliqué technique of all. Again, your cutting technique is key, but in this case you are not trying to cut as close as possible to the stitching. Rather, you want to leave an even width outside the stitching line. There are stitched areas inside the design that, when cut out, expose the first layer of felt through a keyhole to create an added dimension.

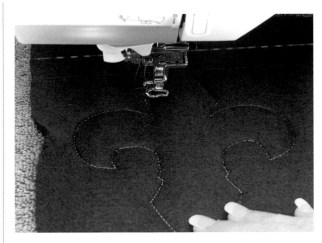

1 Stitch the first design segment—the target stitch—and cut felt to the appropriate size. Apply the felt to the background fabric. Stitch the bean stitch outline of the first element.

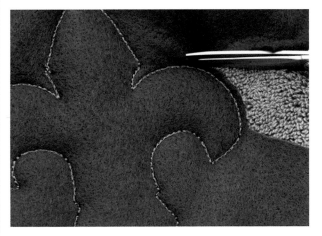

2 Trim the first layer of felt, leaving a ¼" (6mm) margin of felt around the stitching. This margin gives a pleasing look and will not curl after washing.

TIP I specifically designed this embroidery to have the bean stitch as the decorative stitch. It is both a secure and attractive stitch. Notice that there are three running stitches side-by-side. Consider incorporating the bean stitch into other projects that use the raw-edge appliqué technique.

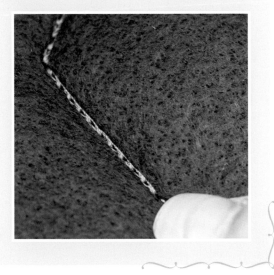

NOTES FROM NANCY

Many years ago, I learned from Deborah and her friend, Eileen Roche, the importance of pressing a light-tack fusible tear-away stabilizer to the wrong side of a towel. If you forgo this step, there is a good chance that loops from the towel will pull a snag when you remove the towel from the adhesive stabilizer.

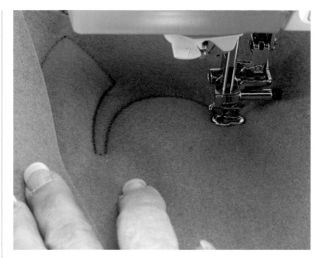

3 Apply the second layer of felt and stitch the second design.

4 Trim out the keyhole portions of the pattern from the second layer. To start cutting these areas, place the pointed tip of your scissors into the center of the keyhole, making sure that you don't damage the felt layer below with your scissors. Leave the same ¼" (6mm) margin or a bit less in these areas. Trim away the excess felt from the outer edge of the second layer.

EMBROIDERY INSIGHTS

Many designs in your library can probably be used to create raw-edge appliqués. For example, you may have designs with a running stitch outline, such as those created for redwork. These designs usually have a double layer of running stitches. Although not as heavy as the bean stitch, many of these can be used for raw-edge appliqué. The shape should be simple enough to cut around it easily. Interior details are fine and can be stitched on top of the appliqué material. You may want to consider using a thicker thread, such as size 30, on running stitch designs.

Traditional appliqué designs may also be used for raw-edge appliqué. Just stitch the target and the cut line on top of the felt for a double layer, omitting the tackdown and satin layers.

STITCHING GUIDES

Traditional Appliqué	**Raw-Edge Appliqué**
The complete stitching guide can be accessed on the DVD under the file name 01_FleurDeLys.pdf.	The complete stitching guide can be accessed on the DVD under the file name 01_Fleur_Raw_Edge.pdf.

LIME GREEN
1510 Sulky Rayon

GRASS GREEN
1049 Sulky Rayon

LIME GREEN
1510 Sulky Rayon

TRUE GREEN
1101 Sulky Rayon

TRUE GREEN
1101 Sulky Rayon

GRASS GREEN
1049 Sulky Rayon

Reverse Appliqué with Fringe
A FANTASY IN THREAD

Fringed embroidery is frequently playful; however, the fringed mane on this giraffe also adds a note of realism. The keys to effective use of fringed elements elude many designers, but this charming fellow wears his fringed mane to good effect. It draws the eye and doesn't disappoint. The fringe is lush and full; the length is appropriate for the subject. Combined with the virtually foolproof technique of reverse appliqué, the look is rich and elegant.

This project is a real showpiece, but even the most novice embroiderer can successfully complete it with ease. In this chapter, you'll learn to love this simple approach to appliqué by creating effective accents with fringe.

NOTES FROM **NANCY**

Before you create this reverse appliqué with fringe, check out the video section on the DVD. You'll hear additional insights from Deborah, and the process will become crystal clear!

REVERSE APPLIQUÉ WITH FRINGE

materials

12" (30.5cm) square of small-scale giraffe print fabric

Durable fabric sufficient to re-cover footstool (faux leather or vinyl are not suitable)

Small footstool that can be re-covered

Size-40 rayon or polyester embroidery thread

Size 75/11 embroidery needles

Sharp, short-blade scissors

Embroidery spray adhesive

6" × 10" (15.2cm × 25.4cm) embroidery hoop

Giraffe embroidery design (02_Giraffe)

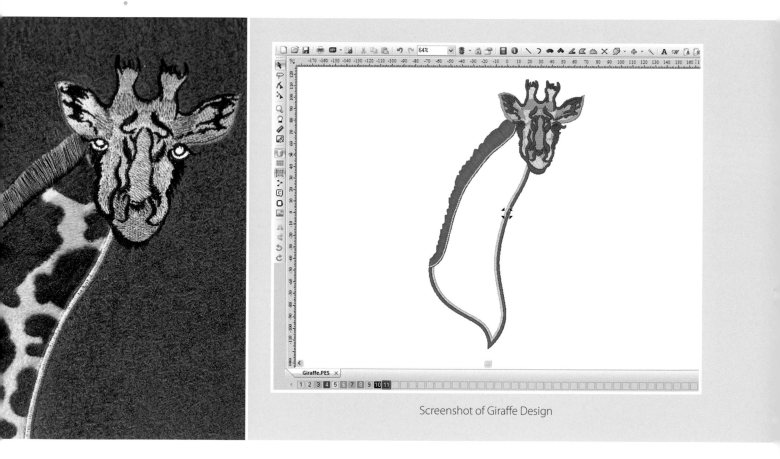

Screenshot of Giraffe Design

RECOMMENDATIONS

FOOTSTOOL

When selecting a footstool, choose one that has appropriate dimensions and style to complement the giraffe design. A footstool with a leaf motif in the metal or an African style footstool in a small square or oblong shape will work well.

FABRIC

Use a fabric that will be durable but will not show needle holes. After the fringe has been cut free, the holes along the outside edge will be exposed. Vinyl, leather or faux leather will not close up around these holes, and they will be permanently visible. In this project, I used a bonded fabric called Elephant Dot, because it has a surface texture that helps to disguise any marks that could remain from the holes. Be sure to select a fabric that can be hooped.

The fabric that will be used for the reverse appliqué should have giraffe spots in a scale that is appropriate for the size of the design. Print the giraffe template from the stitching guide file on the DVD. Cut a window in the neck of the giraffe on the template and take it to the fabric store to preview fabrics for the appliqué. The fabric type is not as important as the proper scale. The fabric may be plush, a polyester/cotton blend or almost any type that is compatible with the color of the top fabric and the design. You may wish to apply a fusible stabilizer to the reverse side of the appliqué fabric if it is a type that frays easily. This will make your footstool more serviceable.

Giraffe Footstool

1 Hoop the top fabric very securely because you will be removing the hoop to cut the window and apply the fabric. If your hoop type allows it, recess the inner hoop so it sits slightly lower than the outer hoop. This will keep your hoop secure and reduce the risk that the fabric will pop out.

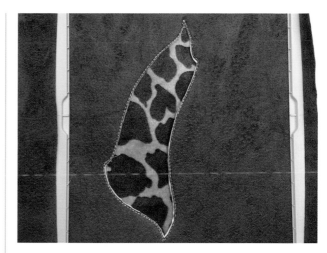

5 Replace the hoop in the machine. Stay with the machine while the running stitch tacks the appliqué fabric to the top fabric. Watch to make sure that the embroidery foot doesn't get caught under the opening edge. If this occurs, stop the machine, release the top fabric and restart the machine.

2 Stitch the first color, a running stitch cutting line. Cut inside the line to form the window for the reverse appliqué.

3 Move the fabric around under the opening to find the best position for the pattern.

4 Secure the appliqué fabric to the reverse side of the top fabric with embroidery spray adhesive. It's best to place the hooped fabric inside a large box away from the embroidery machine. Spray around the edges of the opening and finger press the appliqué fabric to the adhesive, taking care not to loosen the top fabric in the hoop.

6 Stitch the satin stitch outer border.

7 Apply wide satin stitches at the back of the neck to form the fringe for the mane. Finish sewing the mane and the running stitch at the base of the mane and remove the hoop from the machine. From the top, slide small, sharp scissors under the outside edge of the satin stitches to cut the fringe for the mane.

Some designers who create fringe designs recommend cutting the bobbin thread to release the top thread and create the fringe. This method creates a hook on the top thread where it has entered the fabric. The fringe created by this method normally needs to be trimmed to remove this hook. In my opinion, it's best to cut the fringe from the top of the fabric, eliminating the need to trim the fringe. For added security, fuse a piece of fusible stabilizer such as Tender Touch to the reverse side of the fringe.

8 To finish the design, stitch the head. Remove the hoop and trim the appliqué fabric about ¼" (6mm) from the edge of the stitching.

9 Cover the footstool. It may not be necessary to remove the original cover from the footstool in order to re-cover it. If the style of your footstool allows, use a staple gun or hot glue gun to attach the new cover, leaving the original cover in place.

EMBROIDERY INSIGHTS

To create your own fringe designs, look for themes that would be complemented by fringe. The fringed elements could be a mane as in the giraffe, fur, feathers or purely a fantasy element. For example, some designers have created floral designs using fringed elements. One of the challenges with creating fringe is that the fringe stitches should be no longer than 11 millimeters, slightly less than ½". Most machine manufacturers recommend that stitches should not exceed this length.

For this reason, scale is important. The fringed element must look in scale and be no more than this length. Of course, the fringe could be shorter, but in developing fringe designs of my own, I find that the stitch length limitation is frequently an issue. A good example is that the stitch length does not allow for a realistic horse mane, yet it's perfect for a zebra.

Another consideration is that the thread will untwist through laundering and wear. This results in the fringed element looking fluffier over time. For most designs, this is a plus, because you usually want your fringe to look lush, not thin. For this reason, you should probably digitize two layers of satin stitches to create the fringe, with a double running stitch along one side to anchor the stitches after they have been cut. Be sure that the running stitches stitch on top of the satin stitch rather than beside them. This is the key to the fringe technique.

STITCHING GUIDE

Giraffe

The complete stitching guide can be accessed on the DVD under the file name 02_Giraffe.pdf.

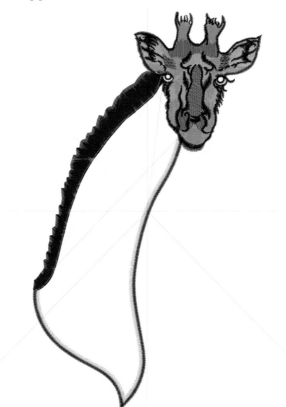

1
DEEP ECRU
1149 Sulky Rayon

5
DK ECRU
1128 Sulky Rayon

9
DK ECRU
1128 Sulky Rayon

2
DEEP ECRU
1149 Sulky Rayon

6
APRICOT
1239 Sulky Rayon

10
SOFT WHITE
1002 Sulky Rayon

3
DEEP ECRU
1149 Sulky Rayon

7
DK ECRU
1128 Sulky Rayon

11
BLACK
1005 Sulky Rayon

4
MED MAPLE
1216 Sulky Rayon

8
MED MAPLE
1216 Sulky Rayon

Appliqué with Lifelike Fur:
EMBROIDERY COMES TO LIFE

There are many types of materials that can be used for appliqué and many reasons to choose one over another. Some fabrics add a touch of fantasy or whimsy to a piece, but in this project I chose a material that adds realism.

The beautiful elk design is enhanced with an appliqué that is mostly covered in a light layer of stitching. Just enough of the plush material peeks through the stitches to make the elk look like it just stepped into the meadow.

In this project, you will see how this technique can add lushness to designs. For covered fur appliqué to be at its most effective, it must be subtle. Exposing too much fur, or using fur or pile fabric that is too long, looks fake rather than intriguing. When you create this project, you will see how adding a little fur under the stitches can bring your embroidered animals to life.

APPLIQUÉ with LIFELIKE FUR

materials

Low-pile faux fur or plush fabric

Throw blanket or other embroidery background

Stabilizer suited to your selected embroidery background

Rayon, polyester or cotton embroidery thread

Standard embroidery needles

Sharp, short-blade scissors

Personal trimmers, electric hair trimmers or animal clippers

8" × 8" (20.3cm × 20cm) or 6" × 10" (15.2cm × 25.4cm) embroidery hoop

Elk embroidery design (03_Elk)

Screenshot of Elk Design

RECOMMENDATIONS

FABRIC

The fur fabric for this elk design should be light tan in color. Most of the fabrics that I tested had fur that was too long. Although this can be shortened with the trimmers, it's best to begin with a fairly short pile fabric. I actually got my pile fabric from an old teddy bear! It was the perfect color and almost the perfect length. The color of my faux fur is a honey beige, but a slightly lighter or darker color would also work.

Selecting the proper pile fabric and having a properly digitized design are the keys to making fur appliqué technique work well. The height of the pile should be similar to the height of a velvet pile. Plush fabrics do not have a pile that is upright like velvet, so it is important to position the pile so that it faces the direction that the animal's hair would grow. In the case of the elk design, the pile should face downward.

I chose the green throw blanket because it was made from a faux suede material with a faux sheepskin trim. It seemed perfect for my elk design because the texture of the faux suede comple-mented the texture of the fur on the elk.

THREAD

Thread colors should also be carefully chosen for this design. The fur is intended to add to the realism of the elk, so don't let choice of thread colors detract from it.

DIGITIZING

Proper digitizing is essential because there is a narrow window of density that will allow the right amount of fur to show through. Too much fur looks cheesy and unrealistic. The only stitches where fur comes through are fill-stitched areas. Where the fur should show through the density of the fill-stitched areas is much looser than a typical design area. In the elk design, the density setting in the fill-stitched areas over the fur is 9 points as compared to a more standard setting of 3 to 4 points. In fill-stitched areas, this value is a measurement of the distance between the rows of stitches; a larger number indicates more distance between the rows. Satin stitched areas are digitized at regular density value of 3 or 4 points.

Cozy Elk Blanket

1 Start by preparing your appliqué material. The nap is too high on my fabric, so I am shaving it down to a length similar to short velvet. A pile that is too high can be pushed in different directions by the presser foot, creating an uneven and messy appearance.

3 Lay the fur over the target stitch. If your pile fabric has a directional pile, place the pile facing downward. Stitch the tackdown stitch and carefully remove the hoop from the machine. Using short blade embroidery scissors, trim close to the edge of the tackdown stitching line.

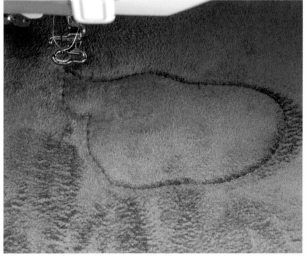

2 Hoop the background fabric and stitch the target stitch.

Be sure to orient the nap of the fabric so the fur appears the way it would grow on the animal. Pet the fur, making certain that it will lay smooth side down from the spine to the legs.

NOTES FROM **NANCY**

An optional fabric for the appliqué would be faux suede in a medium brown or taupe shade. Ultrasuede and Sensuede don't have the nap of fur yet would be great alternatives for this project.

4 Replace the hoop into the machine and place the light-density fill stitches over the fur. Stay near the machine until the fur portion has been completed. Stitch the tackdown stitch around the edges of the appliqué fabric. Begin to stitch the light-density fill over the fur. Continue stitching the entire design.

EMBROIDERY INSIGHTS

If you have experience with embroidery editing software, you can edit your own wildlife and other animal designs for use with fur-covered appliqué. The best candidates are animals with a good-sized area of fill. A satin stitched border is not necessary. It's also helpful if the design has a layer of underlay or perimeter stitch to help you position your appliqué piece properly. The density of the fur-covered area in the elk is 9 points, but you may need to experiment with various densities to achieve the desired effect for your particular animal and design size.

You may also need to manipulate sections of stitching separately. For example, if you wanted to put white fur under a black-and-white, long-haired dog, you could loosen the density on the white fill stitches and leave the density on the black areas at the normal density setting. In this way, the black areas will keep their proper color.

STITCHING GUIDE

Elk

The complete stitching guide can be accessed on the DVD under the file name 03_Elk.pdf.

1
MED ECRU
1127 Sulky Rayon

2
MED ECRU
1127 Sulky Rayon

3
MED ECRU
1127 Sulky Rayon

4
MED ECRU
1127 Sulky Rayon

5
MED ECRU
1127 Sulky Rayon

6
MED ECRU
1127 Sulky Rayon

7
CHESTNUT
1217 Sulky Rayon

8
DK TAWNY TAN
1057 Sulky Rayon

9
DK TAWNY TAN
1057 Sulky Rayon

10
FLAX
1549 Sulky Rayon

11
FLAX
1549 Sulky Rayon

12
DK ECRU
1128 Sulky Rayon

13
DK TAWNY TAN
1057 Sulky Rayon

14
DK TAWNY TAN
1057 Sulky Rayon

15
MED DK ECRU
1054 Sulky Rayon

16
MAPLE
1021 Sulky Rayon

Cutwork
A CHARMING CLASSIC

Cutwork has always fascinated me. The negative space created where the fabric has been cut away is seductive to the eye and draws the viewer deeper. That's one reason why cutwork should be executed flawlessly—it's certain to be scrutinized.

Cutwork is a classic technique, and I like to think of my cutwork pieces as heirloom-quality. I consider the finished product as timeless, rather than old-fashioned. The beautiful napkins in this project are intended to grace a formal dinner table, and they are certain to be a conversation piece among your guests. Imagine your guests' surprise when you tell them that you created such an elegant and seemingly complex creation.

In reality, cutwork is simple to execute, but it takes care in the cutting process. I'm glad that I made an "A" in cutting in my high school home-economics class! Be prepared to take your time and enjoy the technique, knowing it will be admired for years to come.

CUTWORK

Desired number of cotton napkins with crochet trim

Small piece of silklike polyester fabric

Heavyweight water-soluble stabilizer

Rayon, cotton or polyester embroidery thread

Standard embroidery needles

Sharp, short-blade scissors

Iron and ironing board

Embroidery spray adhesive

4" × 4" (10.2cm × 10.2cm) embroidery hoop

Cutwork embroidery design (04_Cutwork)

Screenshot of Cutwork Design

RECOMMENDATIONS

FABRICS

The napkins used in this project are a firm-weave cotton variety. This is important because the firm weave will hold its shape after the holes have been cut and during the overcasting portion of the design. You can make your own napkins if you want a specific color, or order white ones (see the Resources section on page 110). The crocheted edge on the white napkins I use complements the cutwork technique. If you make your own napkins, you may choose to embroider the raw fabric and cut out the napkin after the embroidery is complete.

The silklike polyester serves as a reverse appliqué behind the large opening in the design. It adds a surprising new texture and a slightly different element of color. The color of the polyester insert should be subtle because you want the cutwork to be the star.

STABILIZERS

Water-soluble stabilizers come in three basic weights: regular, midweight and heavyweight. You will want to use a heavyweight variety for this project. This is the only stabilizer that will be used, so choose a high-quality, water-soluble stabilizer. The weight should be about 80 microns. Because most manufacturers don't provide this information, check the Resources section for several recommended water-soluble stabilizers of this weight.

THREAD

The thread colors can be adapted easily to any color scheme by substituting a different color family in the values called for in the design. For example, where the dark purple appears in the design, substitute dark blue, and where lavender appears, substitute light blue. The design can be as dramatic or as subtle as you wish, because the cutwork provides the drama.

SCISSORS

As its name implies, cutting is one of the main components of this technique. Short-blade scissors are important to most projects in this book, but for obvious reasons they are vital to this technique.

Cutwork Napkins with Violets

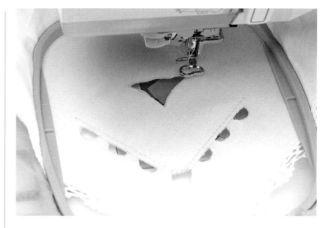

1 Print out the cutwork template from the DVD. Use it to position the napkin in the hoop. The napkin will be hooped "on point" preferably in a 4" × 4" (10.2cm × 10.2cm) hoop. Place the napkin in the hoop so the center point on the template can be positioned under the needle when the hoop is placed in the machine. It is imperative that the napkin is perfectly centered. You can confirm this with the running stitches at the beginning of the design. If these stitches indicate that the napkin is off-center, rehoop and stitch the guide stitches again. Hoop securely because you will be removing the hoop to cut out the cutwork sections.

3 Cut a piece of silklike polyester about ⅜" (1cm) larger than the opening on all edges. Don't make it larger than this, because it will extend into one of the scalloped-edge openings. Don't make it much smaller, or it may not be well-secured. Lightly spray the reverse side of the napkin with embroidery spray adhesive and adhere the polyester fabric with the right side showing through the V-shaped opening.

When trimming small areas, I've been known to place the hoop on a rotary cutting mat and trim with a craft knife. Make sure you haven't had too much coffee—you'll need a steady hand. Yet, trimming on a flat surface prevents the fabric from stretching within the hoop. Give it a try!

NOTES FROM NANCY

2 Stitch the cutting line stitches onto the napkin. Carefully remove the hoop from the machine and cut away the fabric inside the cutting lines. Cut out the large V-shaped section and the semi-oval scallop openings along the pattern's edge.

4 Continue with the embroidery. The next stitches will cover the edges of the cutwork portions of the pattern. Place the hoop back in the machine and continue stitching. If you have cut well, you will be rewarded by seeing the edges wrapped prettily in thread.

6 When the design is complete, remove the hoop and pull the napkin away from the stabilizer base. Cut away the excess polyester on the reverse side of the napkin and press on the right side.

5 Complete the design. After the cut edges have all been covered, the colored floral portion of the design will be stitched. This can be stitched with bright or subtle colors to match your home's color scheme, always with pleasing results.

EMBROIDERY INSIGHTS

To take this theme further, the design will also look great on the pointed ends of a table runner or bell pull or on the corners of a table cover. Always test the design on the same or similar fabric to determine its suitability for the cutwork technique.

Care for your cutwork creations as you would care for any fine delicate linens. Wash them gently in a basin and air-dry.

STITCHING GUIDE

Cutwork

The complete stitching guide can be accessed on the DVD under the file name 04_Cutwork.pdf.

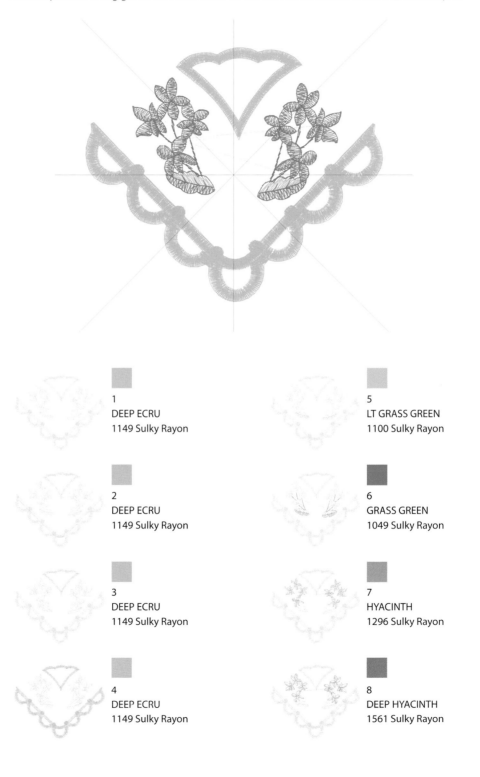

1 DEEP ECRU 1149 Sulky Rayon		5 LT GRASS GREEN 1100 Sulky Rayon	
2 DEEP ECRU 1149 Sulky Rayon		6 GRASS GREEN 1049 Sulky Rayon	
3 DEEP ECRU 1149 Sulky Rayon		7 HYACINTH 1296 Sulky Rayon	
4 DEEP ECRU 1149 Sulky Rayon		8 DEEP HYACINTH 1561 Sulky Rayon	

Lace:
ROMANCING THE THREAD

Lace is perhaps the most romantic of all embroidery techniques. It evokes a nostalgic feeling in almost everyone, possibly because of childhood memories of lace dresser scarves or doilies at Grandmother's house. Grandmother's lace was crafted by hand, and we are fortunate to be able to replicate the look and feel using a computerized embroidery machine.

Lace designs can be delicate or bold, and, like snowflakes, each makes its own unique statement. Handwork lace artisans were highly skilled and, similarly, it takes a skilled embroidery artist to digitize machine-embroidered lace designs. Despite its light-and-airy appearance, lace depends on structure and underlayers that keep it intact. With a well-constructed design, anyone can make a machine-embroidered lace creation.

LACE

materials

30- or 40-weight rayon, polyester or cotton embroidery thread

Heat-soluble film stabilizer, mesh water-soluble stabilizer or heavy-weight water-soluble film stabilizer

Size 75/11 embroidery needles

Sharp, short-blade scissors

Iron and ironing board (for heat-soluble stabilizer)

Water and bowl or pan (for water-soluble stabilizer)

Black tea (optional)

4" × 4" (10.2cm × 10.2cm) machine embroidery hoop

Lace embroidery design (05_Coaster)

Screenshot of Lace Design

RECOMMENDATIONS

THREAD

The lace design included on your DVD can be embroidered with rayon, polyester or cotton thread. Cotton thread tends to give more of a handmade appearance, and either cotton or rayon can be easily tea-dyed upon completion if desired. I like to embroider lace with white rayon thread and then dye it or tea-dye it. This gives a softer look than using a colored thread. A slightly thicker thread, such as size 30, can be used for a more substantial appearance. Polyester thread is also suitable; however, the resulting lace is not as soft.

STABILIZERS

The stabilizers used for lace can be either heat- or water-soluble. Because lace has many connecting elements, be sure to use a soluble stabilizer that is not likely to break down during embroidery. Heat-soluble is somewhat thinner than heavyweight water-soluble, but it can be used in layers. Heavyweight film-type water-soluble stabilizers, about 80 microns, work well for the lace designs on your DVD. Mesh water-soluble stabilizers are a good choice if you see that your film type is breaking down prematurely.

DIGITIZING

Lace can be delicate, but it should also be durable. Digitizing lace designs requires detailed planning to assure that all sections include appropriate underlayers and structure as well as a minimum of trimming. Ideally, a well-planned lace design should not require manual trimming. Rather, it should be mapped so that the needle remains in the stabilizer. When planning your digitizing path, imagine that you must "draw" the design without lifting your pencil. This will help you plan a path that will not require you to use jump stitches to travel.

Lace Coasters

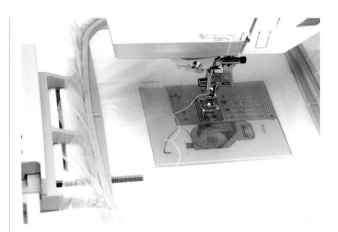

1 Hoop one layer of heavyweight water-soluble film, water-soluble mesh or two or three layers of heat-soluble film stabilizer. Make sure that the selected stabilizer will support the design without breaking down before the design is complete. If you are in doubt, select a heavier stabilizer or use more layers. Make sure that the stabilizer is very secure in the hoop. Poor alignment of design elements in a lace pattern can cause it to be disconnected. Place the hoop in the machine.

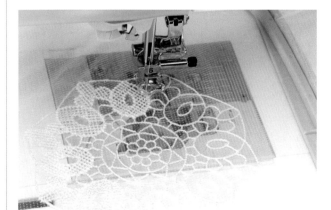

2 Begin with a completely filled bobbin. Make sure you have a sufficient supply of your selected thread color and type to complete the design without cutting it close. Begin stitching. The first portion of the stitching lays the foundation for the lace, then the top layer completes the lace.

Even though your lace project has only a single color and will stitch unattended for an extended period of time, check in on it periodically. This will help ensure that your project isn't marred or ruined by an undetected thread break or other stitching issue. Even though you can back up to the place where the thread broke, the stabilizer will be perforated and will no longer support the design.

3 Remove the hoop from the machine. Punch out the lace from the stabilizer as you would punch out a paper doll.

NOTES FROM NANCY

If you're making multiple lace embroideries, check the bobbin before starting a new design. It's inconvenient to fill another bobbin halfway through the project. In addition, the thread tails would be evident in the design. "An ounce of prevention . . . ."

4 If using heat-soluble stabilizer, place a pressing sheet on the ironing board and sandwich the lace between two coffee filters. Press with a dry iron to remove remnants of the stabilizer. Lift the iron frequently to prevent scorching the lace. Press until the stabilizer melts out of the lace.

If you embroidered on water-soluble stabilizer, I recommend that you punch out the lace from the stabilizer and place the lace in boiling water. This removes the stabilizer the most quickly and with the least disturbance to the structure of the lace. Place the lace on an absorbent towel and gently roll up the towel to absorb the excess moisture. Unroll the towel and allow the lace to dry fully. This results in the softest lace, leaving no stiff, glue-like residue behind. If you are embroidering lots of lace, empty the pot or bowl and replenish with fresh water between batches. Allow the lace to dry, or if you will be tea-dying your lace, do so immediately.

EMBROIDERY INSIGHTS

To tea-dye your lace, boil black tea, either loose or in tea bags, for a few minutes. If using loose tea, strain the water well and immerse the lace. The lace looks darker when it is wet, so remove it when it looks about a shade darker than your desired final color.

Make sure your stabilizer is held very taut in the hoop. The results of a saggy stabilizer will be a disconnected piece of lace, good only for the recycle bin. For this reason, it's also advisable not to economize on stabilizer by embroidering multiple pieces of lace in a large hoop size. After a design has been completed, the stabilizer may pull away from the edges of the embroidery and fail to provide proper stability for the next piece in the hoop.

Always treat your lace gently, and it will provide years of enjoyment. Machine-embroidered lace can realistically become a family heirloom when made using good materials, a good design and sound techniques.

STITCHING GUIDE

Lace

The complete stitching guide can be accessed on the DVD under the file name 05_Coaster.pdf.

1
MED ECRU
1127 Sulky Rayon

Faux Trapunto:
EMBROIDERY REACHES NEW HEIGHTS

Trapunto is a centuries-old technique that originated in Italy in the 1600s. It is a wholecloth quilting technique that involves stuffing or padding traditional design elements such as leaves, vines, grapes and cherries.

The traditional methods for creating trapunto involve stuffing the embroidered elements after embroidery has been completed. Small slits are made in the backing cloth through which the stuffing is inserted. The slits are later closed with hand stitching.

This technique has intrigued me for many years, and I love the idea of giving a design a gentle lift from beneath the fabric surface. The addition of padding gives dimension and personality to a simple running stitch design. In this project, the trapunto technique is applied to sumptuous silk charmeuse using a computerized embroidery machine. Then the design is hand-painted for a robust but pleasingly simple rendition of the traditional trapunto theme of grapes and leaves.

FAUX TRAPUNTO

materials

Silk charmeuse fabric sufficient for your pillow pattern

Polyester quilt batting

Pillow form to fit inside your pillow pattern

No-show or cutaway stabilizer

Rayon, cotton or polyester embroidery thread

Size 75/11 embroidery needles (sharp point preferred)

Sharp, short-blade scissors

Paintstiks (Shiva)

Foam-tipped stencil daubers, round and pointed tip

Small piece of white craft foam (for a palette)

6" × 10" (15.2cm × 25.4cm) embroidery hoop

Grapes embroidery design (06_Grapes)

Screenshot of Grapes Design

RECOMMENDATIONS

FABRIC

The fabric for this project should be very light in color if you plan to color it with paint sticks. You can do the faux trapunto technique without adding color, but I had a lot of fun bringing the grapes and leaves to life with solid paints. A plain, light-colored, ready-made table runner is the perfect background fabric for the faux trapunto technique and makes completion of the pillow easy.

BATTING

When selecting batting, choose a soft, lightweight variety that will allow the silk to remain soft and give only a light plumpness to the grapes. Too much height detracts from the simplicity of the technique.

PILLOW DESIGN

I chose an envelope pillow design because it is ideal for the shape of the embroidery. The bottom of the grapes dip gracefully into the point of the envelope. However, any pillow style that you like will work just as well.

THREAD

The running stitches are friendly to many thread types. Polyester, rayon or cotton thread in almost any weight may be used. Add even more dimension with a yarn-weight thread.

PAINTSTIKS

I did a lot of testing with a wide variety of mediums to apply color to the design, but the silk fabric was quite a challenge. Liquid fabric paint was too hard to control and had a tendency to bleed beyond the stitching lines despite my best efforts to color inside the lines. My favorite fabric pens applied too much color, because I wanted to achieve the effect of a tint or a wash of color.

For silk charmeuse, the only effective means of color application that I found was using Paintstiks by Shiva. Similar in appearance to fat crayons, they are available in matte and iridescent versions.

Silk Envelope Pillow

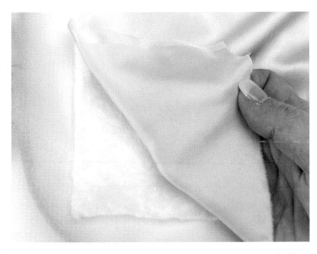

1 Layer no-show or cutaway stabilizer, batting and silk pillow fabric, in that order, in the hoop. Cut the batting to fit inside the hoop between the stabilizer and silk; it should not be captured by the hoop. It needs to be only large enough for the design area. The stabilizer will be hooped in the hoop with the fabric.

Be gentle when hooping this delicate fabric. It isn't necessary for the fabric to be taut in the hoop because the embroidery is a simple running stitch. Resist the temptation to pull on the fabric after you have placed it in the hoop.

2 Stitch the grapes design. The batting creates gently raised areas that will be filled in later with paint.

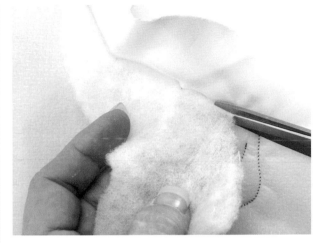

3 After removing the embroidery from the hoop, trim away the stabilizer and batting, one at a time. Always keep the reverse side of the fabric in view to avoid nicking it.

I'm partial to this embroidery design; outline embroidery designs are extremely versatile! Consider embroidering this design on a napkin or incorporate it in a quilting project. As with all the embroideries included on the DVD, there are multiple end uses for these creative designs.

5 To prepare the Paintstiks, peel away an outer skin that forms over the paint after each use. I use a paper towel to peel the skin away.

Apply several strokes of color from a paintstik to a piece of white foam, construction paper or other surface suitable for a palette. Repeat with each color in a separate location on the palette.

4 When trimming is complete, the back of the embroidery should be neat and tidy, with a small margin around the design.

6 Using a small sponge stencil dauber, pick up some of your first color from the palette. Press the dauber against the palette in a clean location to remove all but a small amount of color. Now you are ready to paint the fabric.

7 With a light touch, transfer the paint onto the design.

8 Work lightly and consistently with the paint. Use a light touch and begin to apply the color inside the stitched shapes. You can always add more color, but it is difficult to take color away. If you do apply too much color, as was done here, you can try to remove it by picking it up on a bit of masking tape.

9 While painting the grapes, apply highlights and shading. To apply highlights, leave a small open space on the same side of each grape to represent an imaginary light source hitting the grape. To apply shading, make small areas slightly darker. Because the grapes are round, experiment with using the round dauber in small circular motions. Use the foam daubers with a pointed tip if needed to get close to the edges without going outside the stitching.

TIP Shiva Paintstiks are available in a limited color selection, so I blended two colors to achieve the color that I liked best for the grapes. On the palette, I applied bright pink over a purplish blue to achieve my grape color.

10 For the leaves, you may want to use up to three colors; light green, medium green and light brown. Use the medium green toward the center of the leaf, lightening toward the edges. The brown may be used in very light strokes along the center vein of the leaf. A little of this color goes a long way, so be sure to practice if you want to include brown shading along the vein of the leaf.

11 After applying the color, complete the pillow project. Use lightweight trim to complement the light and airy grape design. If desired, add a tassel to the point of the envelope pillow. The weight of the tassel helps to keep the envelope portion in position.

EMBROIDERY INSIGHTS

Paintstiks can be used to give dimension to redwork and other outline designs. They are also excellent for adding accents to your embroidery designs. There are a variety of stencils, such as leaves and florals, for use with paintstiks. By using these stencils, you can quickly and easily add colorful motifs around your embroidery designs.

I recommend developing your painting technique first by practicing on a sample swatch. This is the most enjoyable part of the project. There is no pressure because it's only a practice sample. After you develop confidence in your painting approach, move on to the actual project piece.

STITCHING GUIDE

Grapes
The complete stitching guide can be accessed on the DVD under the file name 06_Grapes.pdf.

1
CLASSIC GREEN
1232 Sulky Rayon

2
DEEP PURPLE
1235 Sulky Rayon

Mylar Underglow:
SUBTLE ALLURE

Sparkling embroidery is usually the result of embroidering with metallic threads. This specialty thread can be hard to handle and is well-known for excessive breakage. For this reason, metallic thread is often used for small accents rather than for creating an entire design. Imagine a technique that would allow you to add shimmer to an entire area instead of only a small part. By adding a layer of Mylar beneath a specially prepared embroidery design, you can add dramatic or subtle sparkle to a variety of projects.

A successful Mylar embroidery creation will have viewers wondering what it is about your embroidery that makes it irresistibly appealing. Manipulating the colors between the thread and Mylar material creates an infinite variety of effects. It's a fascinating technique for even very experienced embroiderers. In this technique, we will see two of the almost endless possibilities by combining a three-dimensional technique with the Mylar underglow technique to create a moonlit fantasy.

MYLAR UNDERGLOW

materials

½ yard (45.7cm) dark blue silk dupioni, or fabric of choice (background)

¼ yard (22.9cm) light to medium brown fabric (branch)

Mylar tissue paper
 Moon: white, iridescent
 Moth: selected moth color

Fusible stabilizer

Fusible web appliqué stabilizer

Rayon, cotton or polyester embroidery thread

Embroidery needle suited for selected background fabric
(75/11 sharp for silk dupioni)

Sharp, short-blade scissors

Glue dots or fabric glue

4" × 4" (10.2cm ×10.2cm) embroidery hoop
for moth design

5" × 7" (12.7cm × 17.8cm) embroidery hoop
for moon design

Moon and Moth embroidery designs (07_Moon and 07_Moth)

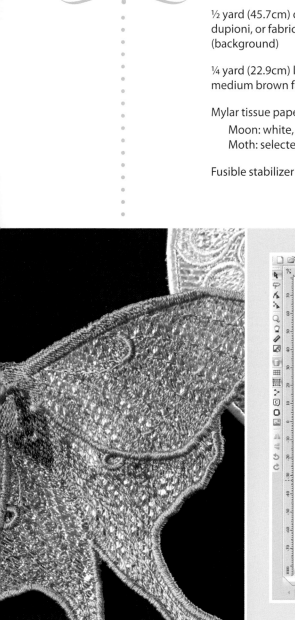

Screenshot of Moon and Moth Designs

RECOMMENDATIONS

FABRIC

I chose silk dupioni for the background fabric because, even though it is a solid color, it has dimension and texture from the naturally occurring slubs in the fabric. When selecting fabric for the branch, take care that you don't use a color that is too dark so it will have good contrast with the dark base fabric that represents an inky night sky. On the other hand, choosing a fabric that is too light in color could detract from the illusion of night.

Cut a piece of your selected background fabric to approximately 14" × 17" (35.6cm × 43.2cm) for a finished size of approximately 11" × 14" (27.9cm × 35.6cm). The moon design will be placed at the edge of the wall hanging, and the extra fabric is needed so it can be held completely inside the hoop edges.

MYLAR

The main ingredient in this technique, aside from a specially digitized design, is the Mylar tissue. This is the same material that is used for the shiny metallic balloons that are filled with helium. You can use the reverse side of flattened Mylar balloons beneath your embroidery. A wider color selection can be found in Mylar tissue packaged as a gift-wrap accessory. It can sometimes be found in a craft store along with standard tissue paper, but be cautious that you don't purchase foil, cellophane or shrink-wrap film instead. Unlike Mylar, cellophane and foil can be torn easily. Mylar is tough, but it can be easily pulled away after it has been perforated by the embroidery needle.

Think carefully about where you apply this technique because the Mylar cannot be dry-cleaned. For this reason, don't apply the Mylar technique to a dry-clean-only wearable. In our project, silk dupioni fabric was used as the base fabric, but because the item is a wall-hanging, it will not be dry-cleaned. You also should not dry items with Mylar elements in the clothes dryer.

Mylar will retain its sparkle through many washings, although the shine will eventually be lost. Because it is a permanent mask beneath the design, your embroidery will still look nice even after the sparkle has diminished.

STABILIZER

Apply a fusible interfacing to cover the entire reverse side of the background fabric. I prefer Shir-Tailor by Pellon because it gives body and prevents the edges from fraying while hooping and handling.

DIGITIZING

The basis of this simple technique is to allow a shiny Mylar tissue to peek through loosely spaced embroidery stitches. The stitches in the embroidery design are fill stitch patterns, rather than satin stitches. Fill stitches are used to cover large areas, while satin stitches (also called column stitches) are used for an outline or lettering.

Luna Moth Wall Hanging

1 Hoop the background fabric for the moon embroidery design, taking care that the moon design will be stitched parallel with the fabric edges. In the case of silk dupioni, the slubs in the grain of the fabric provide an easy reference.

Place the hoop in the machine and stitch the target stitch for placement of the Mylar.

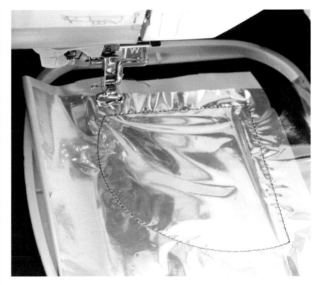

3 Stitch the tackdown stitch over the Mylar layers.

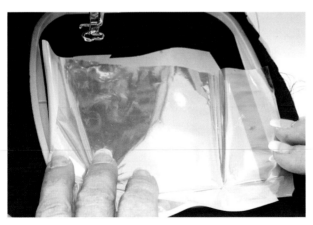

2 Cover the target stitch with a piece of light-colored fabric covered with a layer of iridescent Mylar tissue. The white fabric creates a base for the Mylar so it will show up well on the dark background. When embroidering the moon, I used white and iridescent Mylar. This could be changed to reflect a particular season or mood. For instance, you could use gold mylar with iridescent on top to create a harvest moon. Just be sure that you use a solid color beneath the iridescent layer to block out the dark blue.

When Deborah taught me this technique prior to our videotaping date, I was amazed that I could use the same Mylar paper included in a gift bag as a base for embroidery!

NOTES FROM **NANCY**

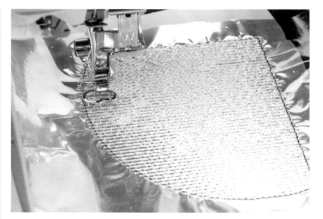

4 Stitch the first color of the moon design.

5 Tear away the Mylar tissue.

6 Continue embroidering the moon design. Complete the design with satin stitches to cover the edges of the Mylar.

7 To create the luna moth, hoop a double layer of extra heavyweight water-soluble stabilizer. Place the hoop in the machine and run the target stitch for the placement of the Mylar.

8 Lay the Mylar over the target and stitch the tackdown stitch over the Mylar.

TIP It's okay if the Mylar gets some wrinkles and bubbles at this point; they'll be smoothed down with the fill layer.

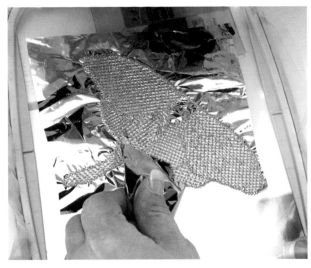

9 Stitch the first color of the luna moth design. Tear away the excess Mylar.

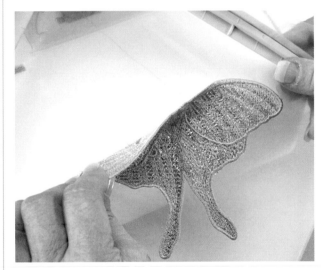

10 Stitch the remainder of the design. Punch the completed embroidery out of the stabilizer and roll the wings to shape.

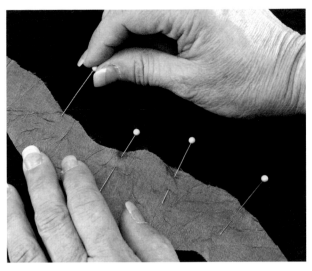

11 Cut the background fabric to 11" × 14" (27.9cm × 35.6cm), leaving a margin outside the moon to accommodate the binding to be applied later. Cut and position the branch and appliqué in place, either by hand stitching or freemotion embroidery.

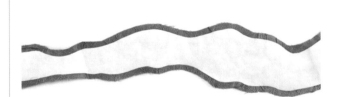

12 If applying using freemotion embroidery, apply fusible web to the reverse side of the branch fabric and iron it into position on the background fabric before embroidery. Remove the embroidery arm or unit from your machine, set a narrow-width zigzag stitch and lower the feed dogs. Follow the edge of the fused fabric branch until all the edges are covered.

13 Your three-dimensional moth may be applied to the branch with glue dots or fabric glue. Apply three medium-sized dots to the back of the moth and place it on the branch facing the moon. This attachment method allows the moth to be removed if your hanging needs to be packed or shipped.

14 Cut strips from the base fabric, assemble a binding and stitch it to the main section of the hanging. Add a sleeve to the back for hanging if desired.

EMBROIDERY INSIGHTS

As mentioned, a design used for the Mylar Underglow technique has loosely spaced fill stitches in the area where the Mylar has been applied. It's also helpful to have a satin stitch outline to help cover any small bits of excess Mylar that may remain after it has been pulled away. Many designs in your existing library could be candidates for the Mylar Underglow technique. If you want to try one of your existing designs, here are some ideas to try.

Good design candidates include fish and seashells. Mylar gives a shiny appearance to fish scales, and you can bring seashells to life with a realistic iridescence. I have used white Mylar under an Arabian horse head design to good effect. In your embroidery design software, open the stitch spacing to 12 points and do a test stitch-out. Leave the satin stitch outline at its normal density. You can select a design with a running stitch outline, but if you do, it's necessary to tear the Mylar very close to the fill stitch. If necessary, remove the hoop and trim the excess so that the running stitch can give a clean finish.

STITCHING GUIDES

Moon

The complete stitching guide can be accessed on the DVD under the file name 07_Moon.pdf.

1
PINK TINT
1068 Sulky Rayon

2
PINK TINT
1068 Sulky Rayon

3
PINK TINT
1068 Sulky Rayon

4
SEA MIST
1275 Sulky Rayon

5
PASTEL PEACH
1017 Sulky Rayon

6
PINK TINT
1068 Sulky Rayon

Moth

The complete stitching guide can be accessed on the DVD under the file name 07_Moth.pdf.

1
AVOCADO
1177 Sulky Rayon

2
AVOCADO
1177 Sulky Rayon

3
AVOCADO
1177 Sulky Rayon

4
AVOCADO
1177 Sulky Rayon

5
CORAL
1154 Sulky Rayon

6
DARK PEACH
1020 Sulky Rayon

7
LIME GREEN
1510 Sulky Rayon

8
DARK PEACH
1020 Sulky Rayon

9
AVOCADO
1177 Sulky Rayon

Silk Flower Appliqué:
A GARDEN OF DELIGHT

For me, silk flower appliqué is one of the most surprising dimensional techniques for machine embroidery. I think of it as a UFO project: it contains Unexpected Found Objects. The blooms, attached with embroidery stitches, may have people thinking you are an embroidery genius, but the technique is easy and is more about scale, color and component selection than embroidery technique.

Your silk flower projects may be whimsical or elegant, but they are sure to be a conversation starter. In this technique, we will complete a charming mixed bouquet using a variety of blossom colors. Be watchful about bloom placement and fabric preparation for a gorgeous garden that will reap a plethora of smiles.

SILK FLOWER APPLIQUÉ

materials

Woven fabric of sufficient size to cover shade, plus 1" (2.5cm) on all sides

Round self-adhesive lampshade (5" [12.7cm] top opening × 14" [35.6cm] bottom opening × 11" [27.9cm] tall used for this project)

Silk flower petals

Mediumweight nonwoven tear-away stabilizer

Fusible stabilizer sufficient to cover fabric

Size-40 rayon or polyester thread

Cotton or polyester bobbin thread

Size 75/11 embroidery needles

Sharp, short-blade scissors

Iron and ironing board

Placement tape or target stickers

Glue stick

5" × 7" (12.7cm × 17.8cm) embroidery hoop

Left Vine and Right Vine embroidery designs (08_Silk_Flower_Left and 08_Silk_Flower_Right)

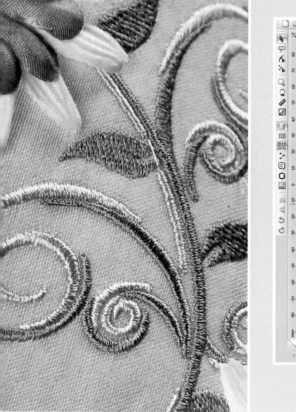

Screenshot of Vine Designs

RECOMMENDATIONS

FABRIC

When choosing your fabric, select a firm, solid-color woven fabric. You can choose a monochromatic color scheme or a colorful combination of brights. It may be a good idea to select your petals first and your fabric second to complement the blooms that strike your fancy. There is likely more selection of colors in fabric than in silk flower petals.

LAMPSHADE

Several sizes of self-adhesive shades are available, depending on where you shop (see the Resources section on page 110). You can choose from larger shades, smaller shades and even straight vertical shades.

SILK FLOWERS

Silk flowers can be used on many items besides lampshades, but make sure that your selected project will not be subject to frequent laundering, like a towel, or to unsuitable wear, like a pillow. Choose blooms from packaged silk flower petals in the scrapbooking section of your favorite craft store, or select from floral stems. Remove the petals from the stems and use them just as you would use the packaged petals.

STABILIZER

Another key to successfully executing this project is fabric preparation. The more lightweight your fabric, the more important this step becomes. I used a colorful Kona cotton for my lampshade, and the fusible stabilizer added much-needed body to this lightweight fabric. I don't think anything beats Shir-Tailor by Pellon for this purpose, but if you have a difficult time finding it, you could also use another lightweight fusible interfacing such as fusible tricot. Combined with a mediumweight tear-away, this should result in a pucker-free cover that can be easily molded to the self-adhesive shade.

Flowered Lampshade

1 Iron fusible stabilizer to the back of your background fabric. Remove the protective paper covering from the self-adhesive lampshade and use it as a template to cut the fabric and stabilizer to size. The manufacturer of the shade used in this project recommends cutting with a 1" (2.5cm) allowance outside the template. Later, this fabric will be folded over to the inside of the shade and glued down. You can serge or overcast the raw edges for a clean finish if you wish.

2 Print placement templates for the embroidery from the files on the DVD. Lay the templates out on the fabric to determine placement for each design. Three designs were used in the example project. Even though the fabric is flat, it will eventually be placed on a round object, making the marking of design placement very important.

Even if you have very good visual acuity for straightness, the templates help you to recall the appropriate direction for each design placement. Print each mirror image version of the stems and label them with their version names so you will load the correct design for each placement.

3 Fold each design placement template in half widthwise to form a straight line. Apply placement tape or a target sticker to the background fabric along the fold line.

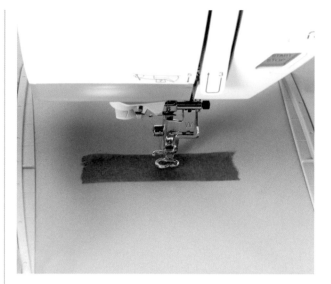

4 Hoop the fabric, using the tape as a reference to align the fabric properly in the hoop. Place the hoop in the machine. The tape should appear straight after the hoop is in the machine.

5 Stitch the stems and leaves of the plant. Stitch the Xs that serve as targets for the silk flowers.

6 Experiment with layering different-colored petals over each other for interesting combinations. If your flowers will be layered, pre-glue the layers together with a glue stick before placing them on the target stitch.

7 The sequence of the design runs so that the stems and leaves are stitched followed by the target stitches. When the machine stops, the needle will be positioned over a target stitch. Apply a moderate amount of glue from a glue stick to the back of a petal and finger press it into position. Start the machine, and the petal will be secured by a round fill-stitched flower center.

8 Repeat until all the petals have been secured. This is the fun part—it makes the design come to life. It's almost like putting the outline on a design that looked like a blob before. As the outline gives form and definition, the blooms make the design come alive.

Your silk flowers should be in scale with your embroidery design. Print the template and take it with you to the store to match the scale to the blossom candidates.

NOTES FROM **NANCY**

FINISHING THE LAMPSHADE

Along one edge of the overlap, press the fabric under ¼" (6mm) and lightly glue with high-quality fabric glue that dries clear. Then align the shade cover over the shade and finger press it into position. Use the fabric glue to continue gluing the fabric margin to the underside of the shade. As stated, the manufacturer of the shade that I used recommended a 1" (2.5cm) margin. While this generous allowance helps assure that the shade will be fully covered, I found it helpful to snip the fabric allowance along the top edge of the shade cover to help fold it inside the shade.

You can glue optional trim along the top or bottom edges of the shade after the fabric has been attached. Attach only 2"–3" (5.1cm–7.6cm) at a time to make sure that it is applied straight. Remember that the embroidery is the focal point, so use a small, simple trim.

> **TIP** Glue from hot-glue guns could become softened by heat from the lightbulb. Fabric glue is preferred.

EMBROIDERY INSIGHTS

You may be able to use floral designs from your design collection by omitting the blooms. If you have design editing skills, you can delete the blooms in your software. Use your lettering capability to insert small Xs as targets for the blooms.

STITCHING GUIDES

Left Vine	**Right Vine**
The complete stitching guide can be accessed on the DVD under the file name 08_Silk_Flower_Left.pdf.	The complete stitching guide can be accessed on the DVD under the file name 08_Silk_Flower_Right.pdf.

1
BRIGHT GREEN
1278 Sulky Rayon

4
BRIGHT GREEN
1278 Sulky Rayon

2
LIME GREEN
1510 Sulky Rayon

5
LEMON YELLOW
1067 Sulky Rayon

3
LIME GREEN
1510 Sulky Rayon

6
LEMON YELLOW
1067 Sulky Rayon

Wing Needle Wonders:
ELEGANT EYELET EMBROIDERY

If you have fond memories of your grandmother's dresser scarves and linens, wing needle embroidery will likely have great appeal for you. Reminiscent of hemstitching and eyelet work, delicate wing needle embroidery looks best on a fine fabric.

Worked with a wide, flanged needle, computerized wing needle work is easy and can be mesmerizing to watch while it stitches. As the wing needle returns to the same opening time and again, small eyelets are formed. Unlike some of the techniques offered in this book, wing needle embroidery is not flamboyant or showy; rather it is understated, refined and traditional. These qualities make it a classic technique to add to your skills.

Wing needle embroidery is easy, but it requires constant attention for the short time it takes to create. It's important to use a standard needle and a wing needle at the appropriate times in the design. Because the designs have relatively few stitches, any skipped stitches or frayed threads are more noticeable than they would be in a typical embroidery design. For this reason, watch as the entire design stitches.

WING NEEDLE EMBROIDERY

materials

Crisp cotton organdy or similar fabric

Ribbon trim (optional)

Rayon or cotton embroidery thread

Wing needle

Standard embroidery needle

Spray or liquid starch

Sharp, short-blade scissors

4" × 4" (10.2cm × 10.2cm) embroidery hoop

Left Butterfly and Right Butterfly embroidery designs (09_Butterfly _Left and 09_Butterfly_Right)

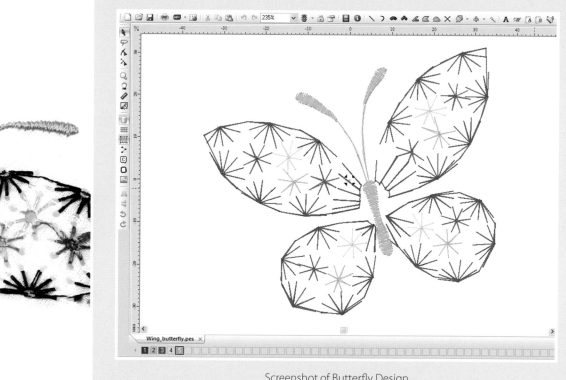

Screenshot of Butterfly Design

RECOMMENDATIONS

FABRIC

The first element that makes your wing needle project a success is the proper fabric. The fabric should be crisp and have a light to moderate thread count. Even if the fabric has a firm hand, prepare the fabric by ironing it with spray starch. I chose a crisp cotton organdy to make my napkins. You can also buy premade napkins with a swiss-dot or hemstitched border. These napkins complement wing needle work and are very inexpensive.

THREAD

I prefer to use rayon or cotton thread when embroidering the wing needle technique. These thread types look more natural and lend to the old-fashioned appearance of this technique more than polyester. For a crewel look, try a size-12 wool-and-acrylic such as Burmilana from Madeira, or a size-12 cotton from Sulky. The eye of a wing needle will accommodate these larger thread types.

STABILIZER

I use no stabilizer because even a lightweight tear-away will show through most lightweight fabrics that are well-suited to the wing needle technique. A stabilizer shouldn't be needed when placing such a light stitch count into a crisp fabric such as organdy. Also, removing a tear-away can stress the delicate stitches. If you believe a stabilizer is needed for your fabric, choose a transparent midweight water- or heat-soluble stabilizer. You may think these soluble toppings are made strictly for use as toppings, but they are also suitable as a backing when transparency is a factor.

Butterfly Napkins

NOTES FROM **NANCY**

When stitching a wing needle design, turn off the thread trimmers on the machine to keep the bobbin threads from being cut too short. (Check your owner's manual on how to make this adjustment.) However, trim the thread frequently during embroidery so it doesn't get trapped under the other stitches.

1 Turn off the trimmers on your machine and place the wing needle in the machine. Wing needles are not made for commercial machines. In this instance, substitute a needle with an extra large blade such as a size 16/100 or larger for the wing needle. You can also use a large standard needle on a single-needle home machine.

2 Starch your fabric and hoop it. Begin stitching the wing needle portion of the pattern.

3 When the wing needle is in place, tackdown stitches are being applied with a wide, flanged needle. For this reason, the tackdown stitches are more fragile than tackdown stitches made with a standard embroidery needle. The embroidery will hold up well as long as you treat the thread gently following color changes. When the machine stops for a color change, unlock the hoop and gently pull the hoop out and forward from the machine. Clip the top thread and gently slide the hoop back and secure it in the machine. This leaves the bobbin thread intact and provides enough slack to allow the top thread to be picked up on the first stitch of the next color.

4 Finish stitching the wing needle portion of the design. Stitch all colors except the last color in the butterfly design with a wing needle. Change to the regular needle and stitch the last color. Complete the embroidery and trim any remaining threads. Look closely at the finished design before removing the hoop to make sure the embroidery is complete. Use the machine's back-up function to repair any defective or missing stitches. Press the finished piece with an iron to remove hoop marks and restore the fabric's original appearance. There will be small round holes in the centers of the starlike shapes in the butterfly.

EMBROIDERY INSIGHTS

Designs can be made with a variety of shapes that allow the wing needle to make repeated penetrations in the same place, creating a hole. This type of digitizing requires careful mapping of the stitching sequence because the thread-cutting feature cannot be used. It's also important to keep threads from becoming trapped under subsequent stitching as much as possible. Watching such well-planned designs as they stitch is interesting and educational.

Here we have made napkins with the wing needle technique. Other projects that are compatible with this technique include dresser scarves, bed pillow covers, tissue box covers and toilet paper cozies. A cheery window curtain or valance would also be lovely with the sun shining through the tiny eyelets.

To make your own wing needle designs, you may be able to use programmed stitches found in many digitizing and editing programs. These predigitized special stitches are used to fill areas defined by the user. Examine the programmed stitches to find suitable stitches that return more than once to the same center point. Also, your design may consist only of the wing needle technique, or it may contain both wing needle and standard embroidery segments.

STITCHING GUIDES

Left Butterfly
The complete stitching guide can be accessed on the DVD under the file name 09_Butterfly_Left.pdf.

Right Butterfly
The complete stitching guide can be accessed on the DVD under the file name 09_Butterfly_Right.pdf.

1
PURPLE
1122 Sulky Rayon

4
OCHRE
1261 Sulky Rayon

2
SUMMER GOLD
1260 Sulky Rayon

5
LIME GREEN
1510 Sulky Rayon

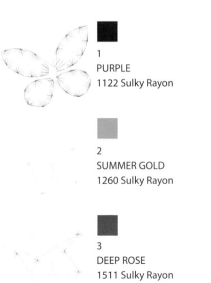

3
DEEP ROSE
1511 Sulky Rayon

Use a wing needle with colors 1–4. Use a regular needle with color 5.

Clear Vinyl Appliqué:
CREATING A WINDOW SCENE

Over the years, I have enjoyed doing many pieces of embroidery using clear vinyl to create the appearance of glass in the design. I have done fish bowls, eyeglasses, windshields and snow globes. The project featured in this technique is by far my favorite because it is so fun and uses a large piece of vinyl, making it the most unique project of its kind that I have created.

The other element that makes this project so special is that it is very personal to me. The basis of the framed project is an image from my front yard printed on fabric. In the instructions, I will demonstrate how to make your window scene with my furnished image or with your own special photo.

The window scene is part realism and part fantasy. The printed fabric and the vinyl glass effect give a sense of realism. The embroidered animals give the window scene a sense of whimsy and warmth. I believe you and your guests will enjoy the view through your window.

CLEAR VINYL APPLIQUÉ

materials

8½" × 11" (21.6cm × 27.9cm) white printable fabric

6" × 12" (15.2cm × 30.5cm) colored or tiny-print fabric

3" × 12" (7.6cm × 30.5cm) lightweight batting

12" × 12" (30.5cm ×30.5cm) mediumweight clear vinyl

8" × 10" (20.3cm × 25.4cm) picture frame

¼" × 18" (6mm × 45.7cm) square dowel

8" × 10" (20.3cm × 25.4cm) foamcore board

Light tear-away stabilizer

Cotton, rayon or polyester embroidery thread

Sharp size 75/11 embroidery needles

Fabric glue

Wood glue

Inkjet printer

Craft knife

4" × 4" (10.2cm × 10.2cm) embroidery hoop

Squirrel, Cat and Bird embroidery designs (10_Squirrel, 10_Cat and 10_Bird)

Background scene (Through_My_Window.jpg)

Screenshot of Cat, Squirrel and Bird Designs

RECOMMENDATIONS

FABRIC

The background scene for this project was printed on printable fabric from Junc Tailor. As an alternative, you could print a mirrored image on inkjet-compatible transfer paper available at office supply stores. The transfer is applied to white cotton blend fabric using a household iron.

The fabric for the window seat can be anything of your choice, but I love a gingham check or small print that has the appearance of calico. Your frame may look best with a solid fabric such as a pinwale corduroy. You can also place a bit of lightweight batting under the fabric to create an even more realistic appearance of a window seat.

VINYL

Find the vinyl in the home decorative fabric area of your fabric store. There are several weights available, and most will work. I prefer the midweight vinyl for embroidery projects.

FRAME

I chose a barn wood frame, although other frame styles would work. I considered other frames for my project, as there are many that resemble windows. I live in the country, and the barn wood frame best expressed the mood I wanted to create.

NOTES FROM NANCY

I have found that some vinyl fabrics stretch or slightly bow when embroidered. As Deborah recommends, use a mediumweight vinyl. Yet, do take time to test-stitch the embroidery on the vinyl you've chosen!

The crossbars that make the frame look like a window are made from a ¼" (6mm) square dowel that has been cut to the proper length to fit each direction of the frame. I found square dowels that matched my frame in a large home-improvement chain store.

NEEDLES

I recommend sharp needles in size 75/11 for this project because they make a smaller hole than the light ball point found on standard embroidery needles. The vinyl will react best with smaller needle penetrations.

IMAGE

The image that I have included on the DVD is correctly sized for an 8" × 10" (20.3cm × 25.4cm) frame opening. You can print a copyright-free image from a stock photo collection or one from a place that is special to you—perhaps your own front yard.

Through My Window

1 Print your background design on printable fabric. The resolution should be at least 300 dots per inch (dpi) for good print quality. If you aren't sure how clearly your image will print at this size, print on paper before using a piece of your printable fabric.

2 Determine the spots where you want to place the small squirrel and bird. Cut away all excess paper from outside the image on the templates and use them to mark the locations. Hoop the fabric and stitch the small designs directly onto the printed fabric.

3 Embroider the small designs (squirrel and bird) in your chosen locations on the printed fabric.

4 Layer the vinyl with the fabric you've chosen for your window seat, placing the fabric for the window seat on top of the vinyl. Use the cat template to help hoop the fabrics in the right place. Also check the vinyl over the printed fabric to make sure the window seat will be in an appropriate location. Slip the piece of batting under the window seat to make it look like a padded seat.

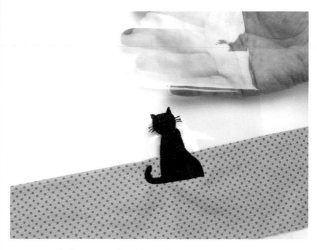

5 Stitch the cat embroidery design on the vinyl with the bottom portion on the window seat fabric.

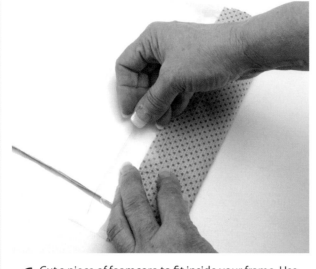

6 Cut a piece of foamcore to fit inside your frame. Use fabric glue to secure the printed embroidered fabric around the piece of foamcore. Trim any excess vinyl and position it carefully over the printed fabric so all of your designs appear in a pleasing way. Wrap the edges of the vinyl around the foamcore and secure it.

7 To make the crosshatch that transforms your frame into a window, measure a square craft dowel against the frame. Using a craft knife, cut one horizontal and one vertical bar to fit snugly inside the front of the frame. Where the two bars meet, cut a recessed area on the underside of the top bar. Secure the dowels with a small amount of wood glue.

EMBROIDERY INSIGHTS

To take this technique further, check out other miniature designs that are available. Match compatible designs to other scenes that can be printed on fabric. I can imagine farm scenes, beach scenes and wildlife scenes that I would love to see through my window.

STITCHING GUIDES

Squirrel	**Cat**	**Bird**
The complete stitching guide can be accessed on the DVD under the file name 10_Squirrel.pdf.	The complete stitching guide can be accessed on the DVD under the file name 10_Cat.pdf.	The complete stitching guide can be accessed on the DVD under the file name 10_Bird.pdf.

Squirrel

1
SOFT WHITE
1002 Sulky Rayon

2
TAN
1126 Sulky Rayon

3
MED TAWNY TAN
1056 Sulky Rayon

4
DK TAWNY TAN
1057 Sulky Rayon

5
CLOISTER BROWN
1131 Sulky Rayon

6
CLOISTER BROWN
1131 Sulky Rayon

Cat

1
BLACK
1005 Sulky Rayon

Bird

1
BRICK
1081 Sulky Rayon

2
BRICK
1081 Sulky Rayon

3
DK SAPPHIRE
1253 Sulky Rayon

4
BLUE
1196 Sulky Rayon

5
SMOKEY GREY
1240 Sulky Rayon

6
SMOKEY GREY
1240 Sulky Rayon

Shadow Work by Machine:
A TIMELESS CLASSIC MADE NEW

Shadow work appears as if it took many hours to create. The faint color showing through the fabric is captivating and mysterious. The methods for creating shadow work by hand and shadow work by machine are quite different, yet shadow work by machine is every bit as lovely as its handwork counterpart.

In the handwork, threads are passed from side to side from beneath the fabric, with an outline stitch placed through the fabric along the edges of the embroidery as each side is reached. The result is that the thread shows through from below and the outline gives definition to the subtle thread colors showing through the fabric. Unlike shadow work done by hand, we can include highlight colors in computerized shadow work designs.

Perfected and patented by Suzanne Hinshaw, shadow work by machine lets us make heirloom creations in minutes or hours rather than days. The machine technique allows for exquisite color blending and intricate designs. As a computerized embroiderer you can reproduce the lovely workmanship of a handwork artisan—in a fraction of the time.

SHADOW WORK BY MACHINE

materials

Sheer batiste or similar fabric, hemmed to 36" × 36" (91.4cm ×91.4cm)

Nonwoven water-soluble stabilizer

Seed beads

Rayon, polyester or cotton embroidery thread

Standard embroidery needle

Sharp, short-blade scissors

Iron and ironing board

Spray starch

Double-sided tape

5" × 7" (12.7cm × 17.8cm) embroidery hoop

Heart Wreath embroidery design (11_Heart_Wreath)

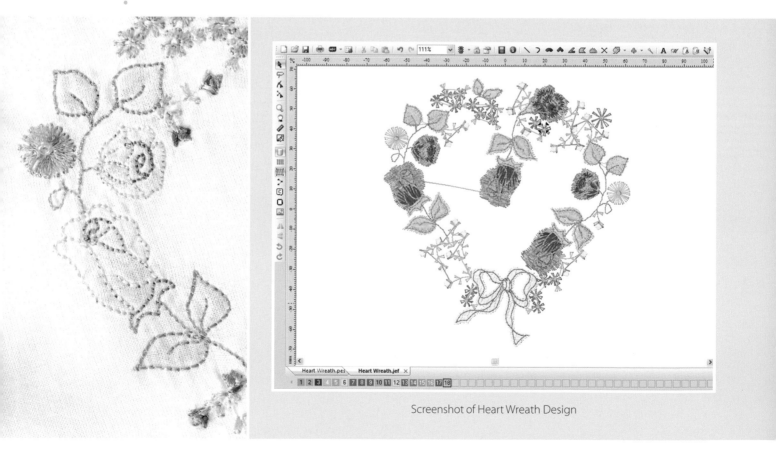

Screenshot of Heart Wreath Design

RECOMMENDATIONS

FABRIC

I used Swiss batiste for this project because it allows the thread to show through beautifully. It also adds to the heirloom qualities of the shadow work technique. Many fabric types can be used, but I find that fabrics woven from finer yarn types give the most pleasing results. Although you can find many light-thread-count fabrics that have a "see-through" quality, some are woven from coarse yarns. The coarse yarn can detract from the overall effect of the finished embroidery.

STABILIZER

I use a nonwoven mesh type of water-soluble stabilizer for this project because it is the most resistant to perforation during embroidery. The included shadow work designs have quite a number of stitches and it's important that the soluble stabilizer does not break down before the outline stitches. It's important that the outline stitches fall just inside the edges of the stitches beneath the fabric.

NOTES FROM **NANCY**

If you selected a more opaque fabric, audition thread colors to make certain that the shadow work will truly show through the fabric. Smooth the fabric over the spool to verify your color choice. This simple test should be a great indicator of the intensity of the shadow work.

THREAD

Any type of embroidery thread can be used for shadow work, but because of the delicate types of fabric used for this technique, I suggest rayon or cotton thread. Using a stronger thread such as polyester could result in damage to the fabric if a stitching problem, such as a bird's nest, occurs and the thread does not break. Metallic thread can be used in the outline stitching for a more formal effect.

Consider the opacity of the fabric when selecting your base embroidery thread colors. The recommended thread colors are applicable for lightweight batiste and other sheer fabrics such as organdy and organza. In this instance, use the same color for the outline that was used for the base stitching beneath the fabric, preserving the handworked appearance of the embroidery.

Beaded Table Topper

1. Hoop a nonwoven, sturdy, water-soluble stabilizer for the base of the shadow stitches. Be sure to hoop the stabilizer tightly, as any slack could allow shifting, causing the outline stitching to fall outside the stitching. The goal is for the outline stitching on the fabric to lie just inside the stitching on the stabilizer base. This ensures that the embroidery is connected after the stabilizer has been removed. Place the hoop in the embroidery machine and stitch the base layer of the embroidery. Clip all threads connecting areas of the design as you embroider so they will not become trapped and difficult to remove.

3. Mark the center of the topper fabric. Position the fabric over the hoop, centering it over the hoop using the markings on the edge of the hoop. Smooth it in place, finger pressing the top fabric to the tape on the stabilizer base. This will keep the fabric in place while the outline stitches are stitched.

2. Apply double-sided tape to the stabilizer base outside the embroidery area.

4 Begin stitching the outline portion of the design. Enjoy seeing your shadow work creation come to life as the outline finalizes the design.

5 Complete the upper layer embroidery. Trim all stitches from the front and back and remove from the hoop. Remove the larger pieces of your stabilizer and then hold the shadow work under warm running water to remove the remaining small bits. Gently massage the back of the embroidery to make sure the remaining stabilizer is completely removed. Roll the embroidered fabric in a towel and press to remove excess water. While it is still slightly damp, place the fabric on a padded ironing board or ironing pad and press, using spray starch. Press firmly and iron until flat.

6 Add small glass beads in complementary colors in the flower centers and other locations to accent the design.

EMBROIDERY INSIGHTS

To take the technique further, originator Suzanne Hinshaw suggests that you experiment with using very soft colors for the base embroidery and soft taupe brown for the outlines. Another color combination that she finds attractive and pleasing is ecru for the base embroidery, outlined in dusty green or silver metallic. Hand washing is recommended for your shadow work creations.

STITCHING GUIDE

Heart Wreath

The complete stitching guide can be accessed on the DVD under the file name 11_Heart_Wreath.pdf.

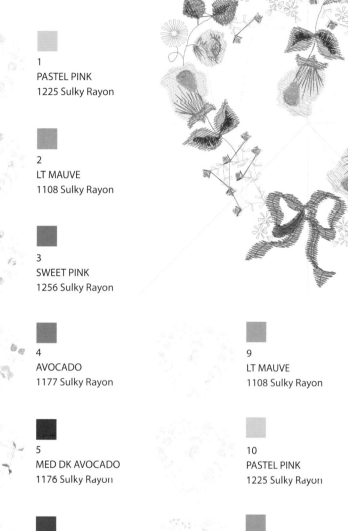

1
PASTEL PINK
1225 Sulky Rayon

2
LT MAUVE
1108 Sulky Rayon

3
SWEET PINK
1256 Sulky Rayon

4
AVOCADO
1177 Sulky Rayon

9
LT MAUVE
1108 Sulky Rayon

14
AVOCADO
1177 Sulky Rayon

5
MED DK AVOCADO
1176 Sulky Rayon

10
PASTEL PINK
1225 Sulky Rayon

15
LT GRASS GREEN
1100 Sulky Rayon

6
DK WINTER SKY
1284 Sulky Rayon

11
LT MAUVE
1108 Sulky Rayon

16
LAVENDER
1193 Sulky Rayon

7
CORNFLOWER BLUE
1249 Sulky Rayon

12
CORNFLOWER BLUE
1249 Sulky Rayon

17
LT MAUVE
1108 Sulky Rayon

8
SWEET PINK
1256 Sulky Rayon

13
DK WINTER SKY
1284 Sulky Rayon

18
PASTEL YELLOW
1135 Sulky Rayon

CONCLUSION

The techniques and projects that we have worked with in this book are ways to expand your enjoyment of the art of embroidery. I hope that the book has inspired you and expanded your view of the possibilities in machine embroidery.

Try this exercise. With each technique, think of a new project that you could make with this embroidery style. If the technique is traditional, such as cutwork, imagine how you would translate stylized motifs using this technique. Think about different materials that could be used and new colorways. Changing the techniques in this book can be a springboard for stimulating your imagination to create your own projects using these methods.

Then, you can start to modify the methods in other ways and perhaps even develop your own. In fact, designer Suzanne Hinshaw developed one of the most intriguing techniques in the book, shadow work, by working it out through experimentation.

Sometimes we discover a new way to do things through "happy accidents". This happened to Suzanne when she was developing shadow work by machine. She forgot to lay her fabric over the top of the base embroidery before a darker color was stitched, and color blended shadow work was born!

Remember that your first attempt at any technique—even one with detailed instructions—may not always look like you want it to. It may be necessary to refine your skills at cutting or even painting to attain the look you want. This is a good thing. You are expanding your horizons and going beyond where you went yesterday with your embroidery.

Whenever someone looks at the projects contained in this book in person, one or more always seem to elicit a "wow" from the viewer. As an embroiderer, I love those "wow" moments. I hope that this book creates many for you.

USING THE DVD AS A LEARNING TOOL

The DVD that accompanies this book contains two resource types: video lessons for several techniques and the designs featured in the projects, plus bonus designs. The video lessons show how to create selected projects, step-by-step.

I recommend that you watch the video lessons before beginning the projects. You will pick up visual tips that will be valuable in your execution.

When using the designs, watch how each one runs, paying particular attention to the stitch types and the stitching order of the elements. Watching for these details as the designs stitch will give you a better understanding of how the designs are created.

If you use embroidery software, you can study the elements there as well. Select a particular object and read your software value for the stitch type, length or density. You can also see details such as the distance between the cutting line and the final outline that will cover it in the appliqué technique. You can gain an understanding of these principles in these properly digitized designs and imitate them if you aspire to create your own. Even if you only want to stitch them, this understanding can help you recognize good- and poor-quality designs when you use materials from many sources.

Use the Slow Redraw feature in your software to better understand the stitching and command sequence. This lets you know what to expect at the machine, and that can be helpful when stitching a specialized technique. This is particularly helpful for certain project types including cutwork, appliqué and shadow work. It will also help you understand how you may be able to convert designs in your existing library for specialty use, or to edit faulty specialty designs.

The stitching guides on the DVD, located in the ColorCharts folder, reference the colors that will allow you to closely replicate the colors as shown on the projects in this book. Experiment with changing the colors in your software to get different effects. For example, the cutwork is in shades of purple. Simply substitute your favorite color scheme using the recommended shade values, such as dark, medium and light.

ACCESSING THE DESIGNS

To access and utilize the designs featured in this book, you must have a computer with a DVD-ROM drive and compatible embroidery software.

The designs are located in the Designs folder on the DVD and are organized by machine format. Choose only the format specific to your machine and copy the design files onto the hard drive of your computer or directly onto a USB drive or other memory device that can be read by your machine.

When the designs are successfully saved to your computer or memory device, transfer them to your embroidery machine following the manufacturer's instructions. For more help with this process, refer to your owner's manual, consult the manufacturer's Web site for updates or contact your local dealer for suggestions.

MACHINE EMBROIDERY DESIGNS

Traditional Fleur-de-Lys

Raw-Edge Fleur-de-Lys

Giraffe

Elk

Cutwork

Lace

Grapes

Moon

Moth

Vine

Butterfly

Squirrel

Bird

Cat

BONUS DESIGNS

Heart Wreath

Basket
Wing Needle Technique

Spring Group
Shadow Work Technique

RESOURCES

AMERICAN AND EFIRD, INC.

www.amefird.com
(704) 827-4311

Mettler cotton embroidery thread

EMBROIDER THIS!

www.embroiderthis.com
(800) 881-8144

table toppers, cotton napkins with crocheted trim

HOLLYWOOD LIGHTS

www.hollywoodlightscrafts.com
(715) 834-8707

self-adhesive lampshades

JUNE TAILOR, INC.

www.junetailor.com
(262) 644-5288

printable fabric

MOONDANCE COLOR COMPANY

www.moondancecolor.com
(508) 847-7493

felted wool

PELLON

www.pellonideas.com
(727) 388-7171

Shir-Tailor interfacing; don't confuse with ShirtMaker, which is very crisp. Shir-Tailor is very drapey.

SULKY

www.sulky.com
(800) 874-4115

Sulky Ultra Solvy, Tender Touch, thread

Sulky Ultra Solvy is a heavyweight water-soluble stabilizer suitable for cutwork and lace projects.

Tender Touch is a permanent stabilizer suitable for lightweight fabrics.

THREAD COLOR CONVERTERS

www.embroiderydesigns.com/threadconversionchart.aspx

www.sulky.com/scripts/colors/colors.php

WHERE TO FIND

Foamcore Board
Find foamcore board in art supply, office supply or large craft stores.

Paintstiks
Shiva Artist's Paintstiks can be found in fine art supply stores. If you have trouble finding them, try searching online retailers.

Silk Flowers
Find jars of petals in the scrapbooking or bridal section of your local craft store or remove petals from silk flowers sold on stems.

Vinyl
Find vinyl in an upholstery supply store or the upholstery section of your local fabric store.

INDEX

More embroidery inspiration . . .

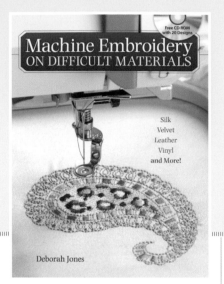

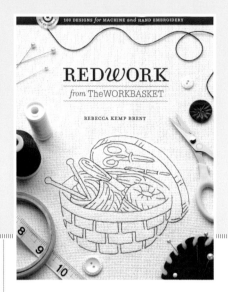

MACHINE EMBROIDERY ON DIFFICULT MATERIALS

Deborah Jones

With the expert advice in *Machine Embroidery on Difficult Materials*, you can embroider even the most challenging materials with consistently beautiful results. Tackle unstable fabrics, densely woven fabrics, and even vinyl, faux suede and leather. This complete reference recommends the best needles, stabilizers and hooping methods for each fabric. A bonus CD-ROM includes 14 embroidery designs with 38 fabric specific versions.

paperback, 128 pages
ISBN-10: 0-89689-654-4
ISBN-13: 978-0-89689-654-3
Z2050

PIECE IN THE HOOP

Larisa Bland

Turn your embroidery machine into a block-piecing machine! Larisa's Piece in the Hoop™ technique results in fast, precise blocks every time. Just add fabric and flip—the embroidery machine does all the sewing for you! The book features step-by-step instructions for 20 quilt projects and 40 designs, as well as great bonus tips and advice from sewing expert Nancy Zieman. An exclusive DVD hosted by Nancy shows Larisa's techniques in action.

paperback, 128 pages
ISBN-10: 1-4402-0356-3
ISBN-13: 978-1-4402-0356-5
Z4957

REDWORK FROM THE WORKBASKET

Rebecca Kemp Brent

Redwork from the WORKBASKET makes it easy to re-create the warm, nostalgic feel of vintage redwork designs on your linens, aprons, even quilts, whether you embroider by hand or machine. Features include a CD-ROM containing 100 vintage designs digitized for machine embroidery in seven common machine formats, 12 projects presented in easy-to-follow steps and a how-to guide for both machine and hand embroidery. All designs also come in JPEG and PDF formats so hand embroiderers can create their own transfers.

paperback, 128 pages
ISBN-10: 0-89689-972-1
ISBN-13: 978-0-89689-972-8
Z3839